SHAZAM!
SIMPLE SCIENCE
MAGIC

Laurence B. White, Jr. & Ray Broekel • Pictures by Meyer Seltzer

Albert Whitman & Co., Morton Grove, Illinois

This book is dedicated to
JUSTIN MARCHANT

We hope your world is always filled
with the "magic" of joy and discovery.
LW   RB

Other books by Laurence B. White, Jr. and Ray Broekel
Abra-Ca-Dazzle: Easy Magic Tricks
Hocus Pocus: Magic You Can Do
Math-a-Magic: Number Tricks for Magicians
Razzle Dazzle! Magic Tricks for You

Library of Congress Cataloging-in-Publication Data
White, Laurence B.
   Shazam! : simple science magic / Laurence B. White, Jr., and
Ray Broekel ; illustrated by Meyer Seltzer.
      p.   cm.
   Summary: A collection of magic tricks exploring fundamental
science principles.
   ISBN 0-8075-7332-9
   1. Science—Experiments—Juvenile literature. 2. Scientific
recreations—Juvenile literature.   [1. Science—Experiments.
2. Scientific recreations.   3. Magic tricks.   4. Experiments.]
I. Broekel, Ray.   II. Seltzer, Meyer, ill.   III. Title.
Q164.W52 1991
793.8—dc20   90-42441
                                                CIP
                                                AC

Science Editor: James Donovan

Text © 1991 by Laurence B. White, Jr. and Ray Broekel
Illustrations © 1991 by Meyer Seltzer
Published in 1991 by Albert Whitman & Company,
6340 Oakton Street, Morton Grove, Illinois 60053.
Published simultaneously in Canada by
General Publishing, Limited, Toronto.
All rights reserved. Printed in the U.S.A.
10 9 8 7 6 5 4 3 2 1

CONTENTS

IT ONLY LOOKS
EMPTY, MA —
IT'S FULL OF
PARTICLES!

GETTING STARTED

Someone famous once said, "Science is nothing but common sense." That may not sound very magical, but believe it or not, science is the basis for some of the most exciting magic tricks you can do.

To the magician's audience, magic always seems mysterious—if it didn't, it wouldn't be really effective. But to the magician who knows not only how but *why* a trick works, magic is just common sense with a lot of fun thrown in. Science magic uses more than a little bit of scientific knowledge and theory to create especially clever tricks.

How to Make the Magic Look Great

A magician has to be skillful at making his or her tricks come across in a mystifying way. One of the most important things to remember is to *practice*. After you practice and can perform a trick smoothly and successfully for yourself, you know it will be a big hit with your audience. Two other important words all good magicians learn are *patter* and *misdirection*. Patter is all the talking you do when you perform; it amuses your audience while you fool them with your trickery. Misdirection is the art of making people look where you want them to, and of course, it's really important.

How to Make the Science Work

The good thing about these simple science tricks is that they use real science, but they're easy to learn! You'll be able to understand the tricks and to practice and perform them soon. You won't need any fancy equipment or complicated methods to prepare your tricks, either. Once you've mystified your audience with a trick from this book, you can reveal the science behind the trick, if you wish. Oftentimes this will make your audience better appreciate the trick by knowing how it works. And it doesn't make the trick seem less fun. Even if the audience knows how a science trick works, it'll still be a source of amazement to them. (Of course, if you want to act like a real magician, keep your audience in the dark.)

A Most Important Theory

We make theories to explain the world around us. One theory a science magician can't do without is called the *particle theory*. It says that everything—air, water, metal, even people—is made up of particles, which is another word for very small pieces. So when someone says a bottle is empty, the science magician knows that the bottle only *looks* empty. In fact, that bottle is full of air particles. When you fight your way down the street on a windy day, millions of air particles moving in the same direction are making your travel so hard. These particles are much too small to see, but they are there all the same.

You can change the way particles move around. For instance, ice is made up of water particles in a formation. They cannot move around, but only vibrate in place. If you take some ice cubes out of a freezer, the cubes will melt and make a little pool of water. Water is made up of particles that move about freely. If you heat the water in a pot on the stove, the particles will move faster and faster. And the faster the particles move, the hotter the water will feel. In time, the water will boil away and none will be left. The water particles have moved so fast that they've flown out of the pot and become a gas—steam.

We'll tell you more about particles later on. But for now, get ready to become a science magician!

THE MAGIC OF PARTICLES

ICE — PARTICLE SPEED ▼ VIBRATING

WATER — PARTICLE SPEED ▼ MOVING

HEATED WATER — PARTICLE SPEED ▼ MOVING FASTER

STEAM — PARTICLE SPEED ▼ VERY VERY FAST

This book is full of wonderful tricks that you can show your friends. But first, would you like to have someone tell you about a trick for *you*—one that would amaze you? Well, we will!

Get a yardstick or a long, narrow board, and prepare to be astonished. Hold your hands as though you were saying a prayer, with your palms together but your fingers pointing straight out and away from you. Now, separate your hands so that they are about as far apart as the yardstick is long. Rest the yardstick across the tops of your hands.

What do you think will happen to the yardstick if you move your hands toward each other? You probably think it will fall, don't you? Well, it won't! If you do the trick right, your hands will meet in the center of the yardstick, with the stick perfectly balanced on top.

How to Do It

Move *slowly*. Slide your hands toward each other and the center of the yardstick. You'll feel one hand move along the yardstick while the other hand pauses. Then the reverse will happen. And keep the yardstick flat—then the trick works like magic! If you want to make the trick look even weirder, take any size ball of modeling clay and put that on one end of the yardstick. When you do the trick now, you will finish with your hands together and the yardstick still balanced, but one end will be sticking out much farther than the other!

The Science Behind the Trick

By the end of this trick you have turned your yardstick into a three-foot seesaw. The seesaw is a big toy that uses *gravity* to work. Gravity is a pull between two objects, such as the earth and you. If two equal-sized players sit, one at each end of a seesaw, and neither one pushes off the ground, they will stay balanced like the yardstick on your fingers. Why? Gravity is pulling down equally on both ends at once. For one end to go down, the other end has to go up—but the pull of gravity won't let it. That's why somebody has to give a good push.

Now, can you guess why a ball of clay placed on one end of the yardstick would change the result? (Hint: think of where the balance point is now.)

Why does only one hand slide at a time, though? Have you ever helped someone carry a long table or bench? The closer to the middle you are, the more of the weight you must lift. Your two hands holding up the yardstick are like two people lifting a long table. As they move toward the middle, one hand will always move a little closer to the middle sooner than the other one. When it does, it takes on a little more of the weight. This hand, which is holding up more of the weight, has a harder time sliding than the other hand. So it stops while the other hand slides. Since the sliding hand is moving toward the middle, it will trade places and become the "heavy-load" hand while the other becomes the "slider." This trading action continues until one hand is holding up all the weight. The other hand slides over to meet it, right at the balance point.

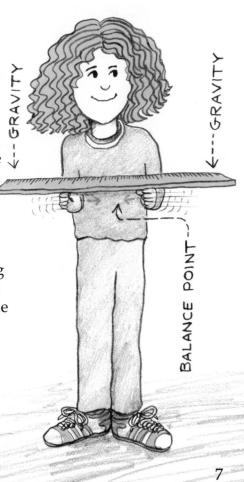

YOU KNOW WHY THIS RULER TRICK WORKS, DON'T YOU? BECAUSE MAGIC RULES!

GRAVITY

GRAVITY

BALANCE POINT

THE QUARTER THROUGH THE DIME-SIZED HOLE

Here's a trick that starts as a joke but ends with you really doing what you said you would. You can get everything ready right in front of your audience. On a piece of paper about the size of a playing card, draw a small circle by tracing around the edge of a dime. Use a pair of scissors to cut out the circle. Have a quarter handy, and you're all set.

Show the paper to your audience. Hold the quarter up to the hole, so everyone can see the coin is larger than the hole. Then say, "A quarter is much larger than a dime, but I can push the quarter through this dime-sized hole without tearing the paper. Would you like to see me do it?" Of course, everyone would. Lay the quarter on the table and hold the paper a few inches above it. Pick up a pencil, poke it down through the hole, and give the quarter a push.

"There it is," you tell everyone. "I have actually pushed the quarter through the dime-sized hole! Now, what do you have to say?"

The audience members say, "Phooey!" because you tricked them with a bad joke.

"Wait," you tell them. "I was just having some fun. I actually can pass the quarter through the dime-sized hole, and I won't play a joke on you. Watch." You fold the paper in half, lengthwise, so the crease passes right across the center of the hole. Drop the quarter inside the fold so it "sits" in the hole. (Of course, the hole is still too small and the quarter doesn't pass through.) Now, hold the upper corners of the folded paper between your thumbs and forefingers. Bring these corners together . . . and the quarter drops through the hole onto the table!

How to Do It

The trick works easily as soon as you catch on to how to fold, hold, and bend the paper. By carefully bending the paper (see illustration) you will find the hole getting bigger as more and more of the quarter shows through. When the hole is big enough, the quarter will drop through it.

The Science Behind the Trick

Because paper is *flexible*, you can change the shape of the hole. When you fold and then bend the sheet, you are changing the shape of the hole from a perfect half-circle to a wide, skinny form. When the hole gets wide enough, a quarter will fit through it easily.

If you want to see how this happens, use a piece of string. Tie the ends of the string together to make a circle. Imagine that the string is the hole in the paper. In its circular shape, it will look like the dime-sized hole. Now, flatten the string circle by pulling it out at opposite places along its edge. The new shape is thin, but it's also *wider* than the original circle.

Now that you know how the trick works, see if you can use your wits to answer these questions:

1. Could you use a rubber ball instead of a quarter? Why or why not?

2. Why wouldn't a sheet made of stiff metal work as well as one of paper?

3. Can you think of a kind of sheet made of metal that might work?

ROUND STRING

SAME STRING FLATTENED IS WIDER

---

3. Aluminum foil.

2. Because you couldn't change the shape of the hole.

1. No. Because the hole always gets narrow as it gets long.

THE ACE OF SPADES

"All of these cards have names. This one I call Wilfred! . . . These are the largest cards made in this size . . . I'll snap the deck two times—that makes the trick twice as snappy."

After some silly patter like this, you proceed to do a trick with the deck you are holding. Set the deck down on a table. "Somewhere in this deck," you say, "is the most magical card of all—the ace of spades. This card is so magical I don't have to find it. Whenever I need it, it finds itself by putting on a big show."

You push the side of the deck with the tips of your fingers so the cards spread out across the table. Somewhere in the middle of the spread, you will see more of one card than of the others. "There it is!" you exclaim, pointing to the card at the space. "That old ace of spades always has to stand out from the rest of the pack." When the card at the wide space is turned over, it is shown to be the ace of spades!

How to Do It

First, take the ace of spades out of the deck. Remove about half the cards and set the ace on the top of the bottom half.

Now, you will need the gimmick—a shaker of salt. Sprinkle a little salt—about ten grains—on top of the ace of spades. Set the rest of the deck on top of that. The cards now look perfectly normal, but there are tiny grains of salt between the ace and the top half of the deck. That is the secret your audience will never see or suspect.

You will want to practice this several times before doing it for an audience, however. It takes a few tries to know just how to push the deck so the cards spread across the table. When you do it

properly, the deck will always "break" widest at the card with the salt on top—the ace of spades. As you show the ace, the salt will fall off and leave no trace of how the trick was done.

The Science Behind the Trick

When two things don't slide easily, we say that there is a lot of *friction* between them. (When they can't slide at all, we say there is too much friction.) Playing cards are smooth and slippery. They slide easily over each other like skates on ice. There is very little friction between cards. With salt added, there is even less friction to slow down the slide.

How does this work? First of all, the salt crystals lift one card off the other so that those cards don't have to rub against each other at all. Secondly, if you looked at salt crystals through a magnifying glass, you would see tiny cubes with very smooth sides. Are these sides smoother than the surface of a playing card? Yes! And smooth salt cube sides lower the friction. So, not only are the two cards no longer rubbing against each other, but the slide between them is increased, thanks to salt's extra smoothness.

11

Do a few swift karate chops in the air as you yell, "Hyuh! Hyuh!" Then say to the audience, "I have this friend who has a black belt in karate. He is a very superstitious person. He says that yesterday he broke twenty mirrors, and that each mirror is supposed to bring him seven years of bad luck. Now he's happy because he's going to live for one hundred and forty more years!"

Now, give a few more swift karate chops and say, "My friend—his name's Willie—does karate with his feet. The other day, I found Willie jumping around in his vegetable garden. I asked him why and he said he was trying to raise mashed potatoes."

You bow to your audience and continue. "Now I'm going to perform a great feat of strength with a trick that Willie passed on to me." Lay a slat of wood on a table, with the end of the slat sticking out beyond the table's edge. Cover the part of the slat on the table with two sheets of newspaper spread out flat. Now tell your audience that you are going to hit the part of the wood that is *not* on the table. Ask them what they think will happen to the paper. Point out that you won't be holding down the wood or the paper.

"I'm going to move my hand so quickly that you'll marvel at the result. So, watch closely . . . I will break this piece of wood without the newspaper flying off the table!" Go into your karate stance. Say, "Hyuh! Hyuh!" and with a quick, downward chopping motion, break the piece of wood in two!

How to Do It

Use a thin piece of wood about three feet long and no more than one-fourth of an inch thick. (A yardstick works well.) Lay the slat on the table with about five inches of the slat sticking out over the edge. Then put the newspaper sheets down—but don't cover the wood that's not on the table. Now make a fist. Hit the end of the slat that is sticking out. The slat will break off at the table edge. The newspaper will lift up a bit, but it won't fly off the table, as you might think.

The Science Behind the Trick

Air particles are in motion all the time. As they move about, they hit surfaces such as our skin or anything else in their way. This hitting of surfaces is called *air pressure*. When you hit *down* on the piece of wood, the newspaper, of course, will try to fly *upward*. But the total air pressure over the surface of those large pieces of newspaper is great enough to hold the wood in place. And, if the newspaper stays on the table, the wood under it stays, too. But the part of the wood that you hit moves freely—and snaps right off.

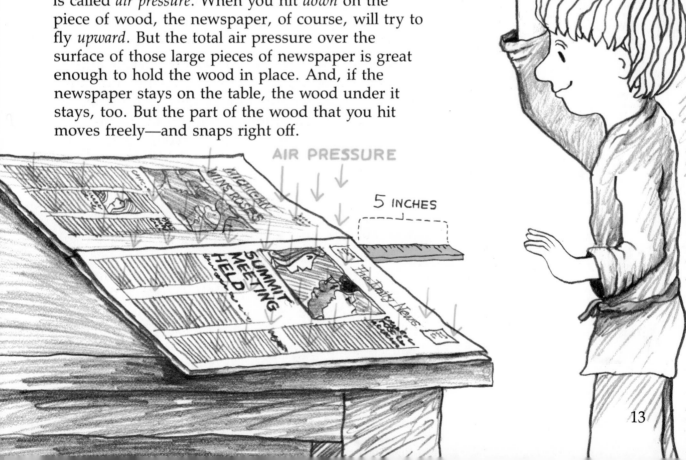

AIR PRESSURE

5 INCHES

13

INVISIBLE THREAD

"People always ask me to teach them how one of my tricks is done," you say. "Would you like to learn one?" The audience quickly agrees that it would.

"I call this the Invisible Thread Trick. First, I balance a drinking straw on the back of a chair." As you speak, you take a plastic drinking straw and balance it at right angles to the back of a chair. Now, pretend to take something out of your pocket and hold it up between your thumb and first finger.

"Actually, the trick uses this invisible thread. I know you can't see it. You're not supposed to. If you could, it wouldn't be called invisible thread!" You pretend to take a length of the thread and tie it to one end of the straw. "Now the invisible thread is hanging down from the end of the straw. Nobody ever sees it, but you know it's there and you can grab it just by reaching under the straw." You reach under the end of the straw and pretend to take hold of the hanging invisible thread.

You're all set now. As you stare down at the straw, you "pull" downward on the invisible thread, and the straw falls! Picking up the straw, you pretend to remove the invisible thread from the end. You pretend to roll it into a little ball. Hand it to someone and say, "Now that you know how to do the trick, you will need this invisible thread so you can show other people."

How to Do It

You do *not* need invisible thread to perform this trick! In fact, all you need is one plastic drinking straw. You can do the magic anytime you have one handy. The trick is in making people wonder if you really do have such a thing as invisible thread. This means you have to be an actor and really look as if you are holding the thread. Make it seem as if the thread makes the straw move, even though it doesn't.

As you set the straw on the back of the chair, try to get as much of it as possible over one side. The straw should be just about ready to fall. The slightest little nudge would cause it to tip off the chair back.

Once the straw is balanced, do two things. First, tell people to watch the straw. Second, position your head so you are directly over the straw and are looking straight down at it. You don't want people looking at your face. While everyone is watching the straw, and your hand is "pulling" the invisible thread, you gently blow downward against the end of the straw! Do not blow hard—people might hear you. If the straw is delicately balanced a very gentle puff will upset it.

If this trick doesn't work right at first, don't be disappointed. Try again. And again, until you catch on. Most magic tricks require practice.

Finally, please only do this once for an audience. If you do it again, someone might catch you.

The Science Behind the Trick

The science secret is that you do not use imaginary invisible thread, but you do use something *real* and invisible—air. Although air particles are all around us, we cannot see them. When the particles move, however, they push against objects, such as the delicately balanced straw. Moving air particles —wind—are the real science secret that makes this trick work.

"Do you know why these pennies are like fruit?" you begin, as you reach into your pocket and remove a half-dozen pennies. You set the pennies on the table. "It's because there's a date on every one of them!" The audience groans at your terrible joke. "By the way, have you ever had your mind read?" you ask. "*You* might enjoy having your mind read, but I generally prefer to have my mind green!" Your audience groans again. "Let's try a little mind reading right now, using those dates on these pennies."

Place the coins on the table and ask a spectator to come up and read the dates on them out loud so everyone knows they are different from each other. Then, turn your back to the audience. Explain that someone is to pick up one of the pennies and look at the date. The penny should then be handed to another person, who is also to look at the date. The penny must be passed to everyone, and each person should look at and remember the date—but not a single word is to be spoken. When all have seen the penny, it is to be returned to the table.

Now, turn around, pick up each penny, and "study" it. Then, turn to the audience and ask them to concentrate on the date. "Well, your minds are read now—because you are all thinking of 1985!" And they are!

How to Do It

First, you must locate half a dozen pennies (or other coins all the same size) with a different date on each one. You can carry the coins in your pocket but, after laying them out on the table, you must "waste" a few minutes. That is why we suggest telling the terrible jokes at the beginning. Perhaps you can think of better ones?

The only other thing you require is an audience. And that audience must pass the coin around. This is one trick that requires a number of people and can't be performed for just one person. Does that puzzle you? Read on . . .

The Science Behind the Trick

Remember, in the introduction, what we said about particles and heat: the faster the particles in an object move, the hotter the object feels. Particles in your hand are warm—they stay in place, but it's as if they were hopping, too.

When you carry the coins in your pocket, they will be warm because they were close to your body. This is why you must wait a few minutes after placing the pennies on the table. This allows them to cool down to room temperature. Then, when the cool penny is passed from hand to hand, the warm particles of everyone's skin, which are vibrating in place, bump against the particles in the penny. Soon, the penny has warmed up. After it is put back with the other pennies, the warm penny's particles will begin to slow down again, gradually enough that there will be time to tell which one was passed among the audience members.

WE ARE THE WARM PARTICLES!

WE ARE THE COLD PARTICLES, BUT WE'RE STARTING TO WARM UP.

17

BLOW ME OVER

"Magic words have great powers," you explain, taking a small piece of cardboard and folding the ends over to make two flaps. "Some magic words are hard to explain—like 'Abracadabra.' What does that mean? And some magic words are just silly, like 'purple-peanut-butter-pie.' My magic words are very simple, but not silly, and anyone can understand what they mean." You write some words on the cardboard and set it on its edge on the table, with the flaps facing the audience. You have written: YOU CAN BLOW THIS CARD OVER.

"I know they don't sound like magic words, but they are," you say. "They will allow you to do just what they say. Try to blow the card over and you'll see." A spectator blows gently at the card and it falls.

You retrieve the card and write some words on the opposite side: YOU *CAN'T* BLOW THIS CARD OVER! This time, you set the card down like a little table, with the flaps as the legs of the table. Your new magic words are on top. Then say, "You know, when you did this before, you really didn't blow the card *over*, you just blew it *down*. This time, I'd like you to try to blow it *over* so the other magic words are facing up. But, of course, you won't be able to do this because of the powerful magic words I've written on top!" Your spectator may now try to blow the card over. She can huff and puff as hard as she wishes. The harder she blows, the more stubborn the card seems to be. This is a trick that drives people crazy!

18

How to Do It

You will need an index card or other piece of cardboard about three by five inches in size. Fold each end inward about one-half inch to make two flaps (see illustration). Then, at the right moment, write your "magic words," as explained above. Once you have everything in place, this trick will just seem to work by itself.

The Science Behind the Trick

Of course, there is a reason the trick works—a science magic reason. There is more air pressure pushing *down* on the card than pushing *up*. This happens because, as you blow on the card, the air moves easily and quickly through the tunnel made by the card. But the air above the card is *not* protected by a tunnel. Air particles outside the tunnel mix with the blown air particles, bouncing against them and breaking up the wind. The slower air on top pushes harder against the card's surface than the air on the bottom because these bottom air particles are moving freely through the tunnel— they're not pushing back!

You can feel the difference. Put two fingers at the back of the card and blow near the front. The tunnel air particles come through with gusto. What about the air on top?

YOU CAN'T BLOW THIS CARD OVER

AIR PARTICLES

AIR PARTICLE EXPRESSWAY NO SLOW TRAFFIC

19

WILLIE'S BALANCING TRICK

"My friends," you say, "—as I hope you aren't my enemies—the next trick I am going to do for you will be a moving performance. I hope everyone doesn't move to the nearest exit. You know, I lack only three things to get to the top as the world's number one magician—talent, ambition, and initiative. Otherwise, I've got it made.

"In the trick I'm going to do for you now, I will use just the tip of a pencil to balance a bunch of stuff on a table edge. Remember my friend Willie, the karate expert? Now, Willie is very strong. In fact, he is so strong that he can tear a telephone book in half the hard way—one page at a time! Willie has two hobbies. One of them is really crazy. He sits around all day and collects dust. The other hobby is more sensible. He balances hunks of clay over the ends of tables, using the tips of pencils. So now, I'll show you Willie's balancing trick."

You assemble the pencil, clay, and fork construction as pictured. Then invite a member of the audience up to assist you. Ask her to hold the eraser end of the pencil and set the tip on the edge of the table, as shown in the illustration. She should keep holding the eraser end. Say, "Now for the magic!" and wave your hands mysteriously around the pencil several times. "Let's see if the magic worked. On the count of three, let go of the pencil. One, two, *three*!" The pencil balances unaided, you take your bow . . . and, don't forget to thank your assistant for helping you!

How to Do It

You'll need a hunk of clay about twice the size of a Ping-Pong ball. You'll also need a pencil, a fork, and a table.

Push the pencil through the hunk of clay. Then, stick the fork into the clay so the handle of the fork points in the same direction as the sharpened end of the pencil. Now, balance that end of the pencil on the table. You'll need to practice this a few times so you know just how to set things up.

The Science Behind the Trick

How in the world can that pencil tip hold up this crazy sight? Let your audience be baffled. You, however, just have to remember the seesaw we talked about in "A Trick for You" (page 7). Once more, you have a game that uses gravity. For the clay and the pencil to fall to earth, the fork would have to be freed from gravity and move upward. But, that cannot happen. The pull on the pencil end is the same as the pull on the fork end. This crazy seesaw is balanced! And that makes your tiny pencil point the balance point.

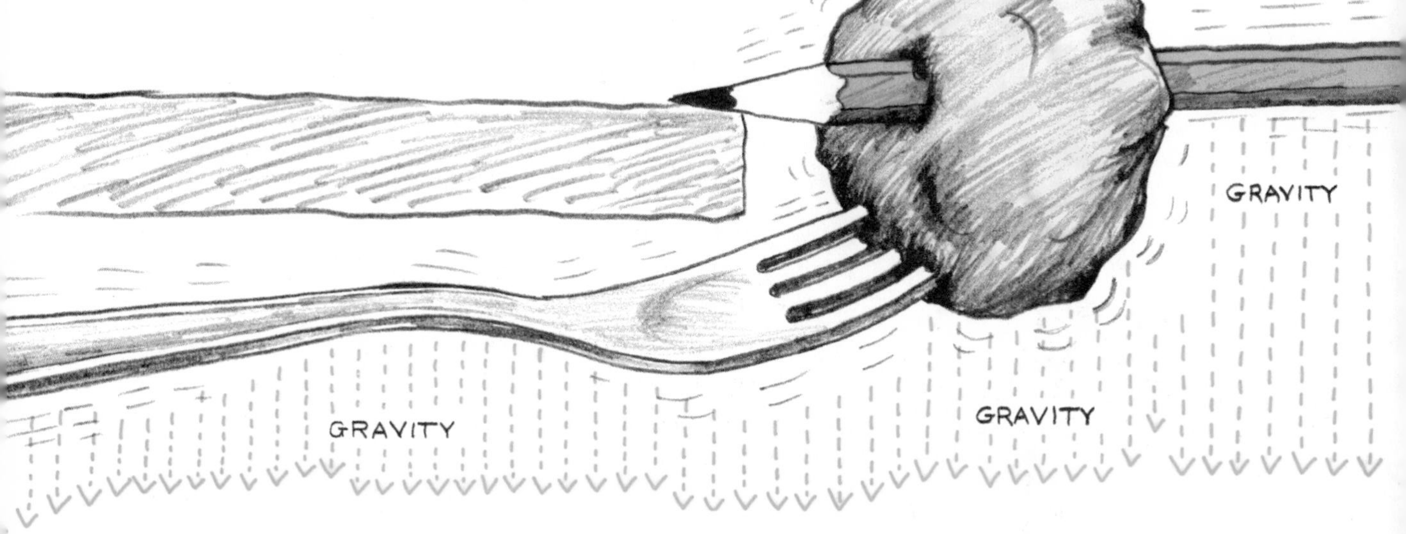

GRAVITY

GRAVITY

GRAVITY

A Taste of Magic

You hand a pencil and a piece of paper to a friend and ask her to write the name of someone who is special to her on it. Then have her fold the slip in half. Now hand her four more sheets of paper; ask her to write different names on each one. When she is done writing on and folding all the slips, ask her to mix them well and hand them to you.

Explain that you will now pick out the one slip with the special name. But, you tell everyone, you do this best with your eyes closed and your back turned. Turn around, and—with the audience watching—hold each slip to your forehead as you pretend to concentrate. Finally, turn back around, holding up a single slip of paper. Hand the still-folded slip to your friend, and ask her what special name she wrote. When she answers, and opens the slip you've just handed her, she finds it is the one with the special name!

How to Do It

You must have five (or more, if you like) pieces of paper. Any size will do, but be sure the paper is heavy enough so that writing won't show through. If you use thin paper, your audience will accuse you of reading the name through it. Remove one piece of paper and set it aside for a moment. Pour a little water in a bowl and put the other pieces of paper in it. When they are wet all over, take them out and let them dry.

Now, add a tablespoon of salt to the water and stir a bit. Drop the single slip of paper in the salt water, then remove it and let it dry. Keep it separate from the other slips. When the papers are dry, they will all look alike. Gather them into a pile, putting the salt-water slip on top. Get a pencil and you're ready to go. The salt-water slip will be the first one you hand your friend, so that will be the one on which she writes her special name. The other names go on the plain papers.

When you turn your back, the audience won't see you stick out your tongue just a little bit! That is the secret. As you raise each paper up to your forehead to "concentrate" on it, just touch it to the tip of your tongue.

The Science Behind the Trick

You have five senses: sight, smell, touch, hearing, and *taste*. People who watch you do this trick will think you use sight somehow because they assume you have to read the names. You are using a sense that goes into action many times every day—one that you'd hardly ever think of as a problem solver. Your sense of taste will locate the salty paper— which, of course, is the one with the special name! Now, test your wits on these:

1. Can you guess why you would need to wet down *all* the pieces of paper? (Hint: What happens to paper when it has gotten wet and then is dried?)

2. By wetting all the slips of paper, what two senses are you trying to get your friend *not* to use?

1. Paper that has gotten wet and then dries is usually bumpier looking than other paper. If you wet only the salty paper, it would look different from the unsalty ones.

2. Sight and touch. The papers will all look and feel the same.

23

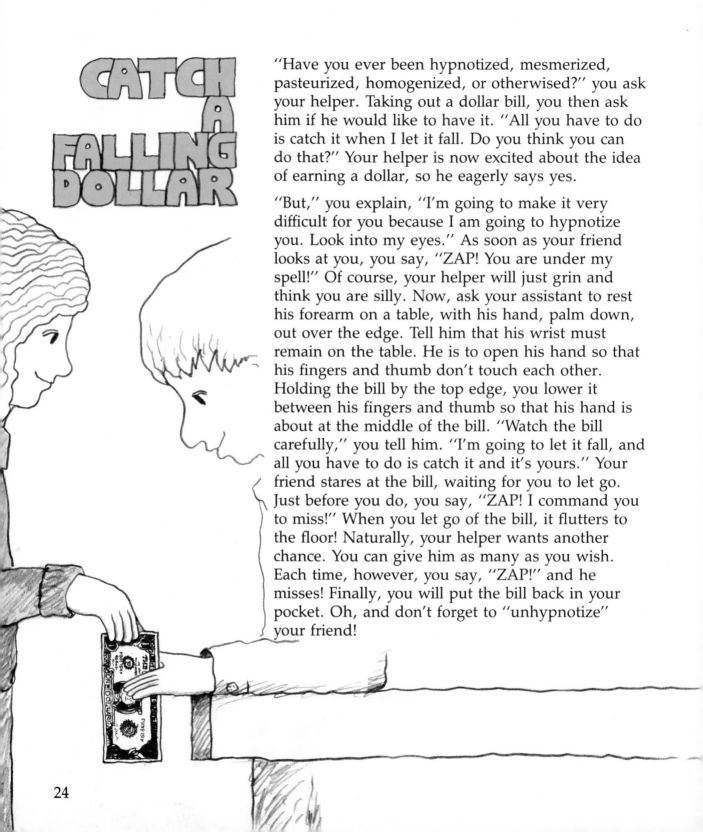

CATCH A FALLING DOLLAR

"Have you ever been hypnotized, mesmerized, pasteurized, homogenized, or otherwised?" you ask your helper. Taking out a dollar bill, you then ask him if he would like to have it. "All you have to do is catch it when I let it fall. Do you think you can do that?" Your helper is now excited about the idea of earning a dollar, so he eagerly says yes.

"But," you explain, "I'm going to make it very difficult for you because I am going to hypnotize you. Look into my eyes." As soon as your friend looks at you, you say, "ZAP! You are under my spell!" Of course, your helper will just grin and think you are silly. Now, ask your assistant to rest his forearm on a table, with his hand, palm down, out over the edge. Tell him that his wrist must remain on the table. He is to open his hand so that his fingers and thumb don't touch each other. Holding the bill by the top edge, you lower it between his fingers and thumb so that his hand is about at the middle of the bill. "Watch the bill carefully," you tell him. "I'm going to let it fall, and all you have to do is catch it and it's yours." Your friend stares at the bill, waiting for you to let go. Just before you do, you say, "ZAP! I command you to miss!" When you let go of the bill, it flutters to the floor! Naturally, your helper wants another chance. You can give him as many as you wish. Each time, however, you say, "ZAP!" and he misses! Finally, you will put the bill back in your pocket. Oh, and don't forget to "unhypnotize" your friend!

24

How to Do It

Have your assistant place his arm on the table with *only* his hand over the edge. This prevents him from moving his hand downward to follow the falling bill. If the person can move his hand easily, he might catch the bill, so these instructions are very important.

Also, be sure that you hold the bill between his thumb and fingers. Be certain that it does not touch the person's hand at all. If it touches his hand, he will both see and feel the bill fall, and he may catch it. Be sure he only *sees* it fall!

If you do the trick correctly, nobody will ever catch the falling bill. (We're sure you know that you don't really hypnotize your helper—that's just a good patter story.)

The Science Behind the Trick

The trick is in how your eyes, brain, nerves, and muscles work together. Just think of what happens as your friend tries to catch the bill: When your fingers open to release the bill, your helper must see it begin to fall. His *eyes* must send a message to his *brain*. His brain then sends a message down to his arm through *nerves*, which activate the *muscles*. The muscles make his hand move to pull his fingers and thumb together.

Complicated, isn't it? It all happens very quickly, but it does take a *little* bit of time. In fact, it takes just a bit longer than the time it takes for the bill to fall out of your helper's grasp. It's not hypnotism that stops him from catching your bill; it's the way his own body works that makes him too slow.

BALLOON IN A BOTTLE

"I'm going to show you something that is impossible," you tell your audience. You display a plastic soda bottle. Inside is a blown-up balloon; it fills most of the bottle. You are holding the neck of the balloon.

"You probably don't think this is very wonderful. You're saying that all I had to do was poke the balloon into the bottle and then blow it up. It's true, that's what I did. But, it's still impossible— for *you*!"

With that, you let the balloon deflate (keep your hold on the balloon neck so the balloon doesn't fall into the bottle!) and pull it out of the bottle. The bottle is handed to a spectator. You reach into your pocket, remove a new balloon, and hand it to her. Then say, "To prove that it is impossible for anyone but me to blow a balloon up inside a bottle, let's see you do it."

She pokes the balloon into the bottle, leaving the neck outside. Then, she tries to blow up the balloon. At first, it seems she might succeed— because the balloon does blow up a little bit—but not for long. Suddenly, your friend is blowing very hard, and the balloon is not growing bigger. She will finally give up.

"I told you *I* can do it, but it's impossible for *you*," you tell her. "Let me show you. I don't want you to see how I do it, so I have to leave the room for a minute." You take the bottle and your balloon and go into the next room. In one minute, you are back. You're holding the bottle, with the balloon blown up inside!

How to Do It

You need a gimmick which is never seen but which allows only you to do the trick. Your gimmick is a plastic drinking straw.

Before you show your friend the trick you must do this: Drop the balloon (a long, thin one—not a round one) into the bottle, keeping the neck of the balloon out. Poke the straw into the bottle beside the balloon. The bottom of the straw should *nearly* touch the bottom of the bottle, and the top of the straw should extend out of the bottle. Now, hold the bottle up to your mouth—but don't put the *straw* into your mouth—and blow up the balloon. You'll be able to do it easily. When the balloon nearly fills the bottle, pull out the straw. Hide the straw somewhere in the other room, or in your pocket, so you can get it later after your friend fails.

That's all there is to it. If you want to feel how frustrating it is not to be able to blow up the balloon inside the bottle, try it yourself *without* using your straw gimmick.

The Science Behind the Trick

Air particles need room. When you try to push them closer together, they push back. But, why don't air particles push together enough to blow up the balloon in the bottle? Because the air particles that are already in the bottle need room, too. When you start blowing up the balloon, the opening of the bottle gets closed up by the balloon. This traps the air that is already in the bottle. As you blow air particles into the *balloon*, the *bottle's* air particles push back! The only way to make room for an air-particle-filled balloon in a bottle is to provide an escape route for the bottle's air particles. The straw does the trick nicely.

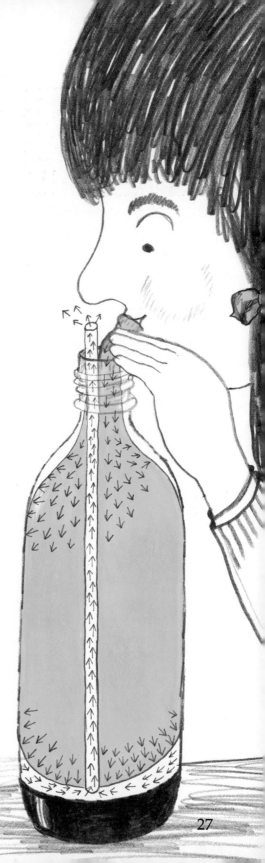

27

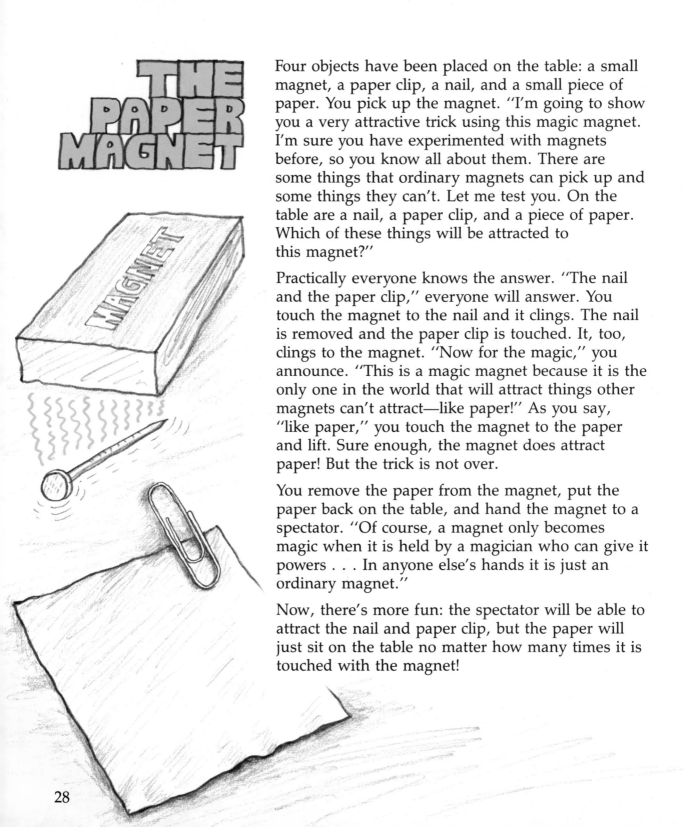

THE PAPER MAGNET

Four objects have been placed on the table: a small magnet, a paper clip, a nail, and a small piece of paper. You pick up the magnet. "I'm going to show you a very attractive trick using this magic magnet. I'm sure you have experimented with magnets before, so you know all about them. There are some things that ordinary magnets can pick up and some things they can't. Let me test you. On the table are a nail, a paper clip, and a piece of paper. Which of these things will be attracted to this magnet?"

Practically everyone knows the answer. "The nail and the paper clip," everyone will answer. You touch the magnet to the nail and it clings. The nail is removed and the paper clip is touched. It, too, clings to the magnet. "Now for the magic," you announce. "This is a magic magnet because it is the only one in the world that will attract things other magnets can't attract—like paper!" As you say, "like paper," you touch the magnet to the paper and lift. Sure enough, the magnet does attract paper! But the trick is not over.

You remove the paper from the magnet, put the paper back on the table, and hand the magnet to a spectator. "Of course, a magnet only becomes magic when it is held by a magician who can give it powers . . . In anyone else's hands it is just an ordinary magnet."

Now, there's more fun: the spectator will be able to attract the nail and paper clip, but the paper will just sit on the table no matter how many times it is touched with the magnet!

How to Do It

Naturally, you will need an iron nail, a metal paper clip, and a piece of paper—about three inches square. You will also need a magnet, which you can buy at a hobby shop or hardware store. The magnet must be the right size and shape: rectangular, not circular or horseshoe-shaped. The size must hide the gimmick. Finally, place a pad of paper, a desk blotter, or a tablecloth on the table where you will do the trick.

The gimmick is something nobody ever sees or suspects: a straight pin. Make sure it is made of steel, which will cling to a magnet. (Some pins are made of brass, which is not magnetic.) The magnet should be longer than the pin.

To prepare the trick, simply stick the pin on the backside of the magnet and lay the magnet, pin side down, beside the nail, paper clip, and piece of paper. The magnet will pick up the nail and paper clip. When you demonstrate this, keep the pin side of the magnet facing away from your audience. As you remove the paper clip from the magnet, turn the magnet so the point of the pin faces downward and slide the pin so the point sticks out slightly from the edge of the magnet. Now, press the pin tightly against the back of the magnet, using your thumb and fingers. Place the magnet's edge down on the paper and push. The pinpoint will jab into the paper. When you lift the magnet, the paper,

stuck on the pin, lifts with it. To the audience, it looks exactly as if the magnet has attracted the paper. Pull the paper off the magnet and hand just the magnet to a spectator. To remove the pin, secretly slide it off the magnet using your other hand. While people are looking at the magnet and trying your trick, drop the pin on the floor or slip it into your pocket, and your secret is gone!

The Science Behind the Trick

This trick fools people because of what they already know. Most people know that magnets don't attract paper. What people do not know is that you didn't use magnetism. That's why you need the hidden pin to squeeze between the paper's particles. These particles push back on the pin so hard that the paper will not slide off. There is too much friction for the paper to slide. So, friction is what prevents the paper from falling off the pinpoint.

Here's some patter to use while getting ready to do this trick:

"Did you know that I'm a well-known author? I've just written something that any magazine will accept—it's a check for a one-year subscription . . . Now, as you watch my next trick, remember that even though I am the world's greatest magician, I don't want you to make a great fuss over me. Just treat me as you would any other great person . . . I used to have an assistant who kept learning more and more about less and less, until now he knows everything about nothing. That's why my act is now a single.

"And now, it's time for my utterly mystifying act in which I cast a spell on this can so that it loses its sense of direction. Which way do cans roll?

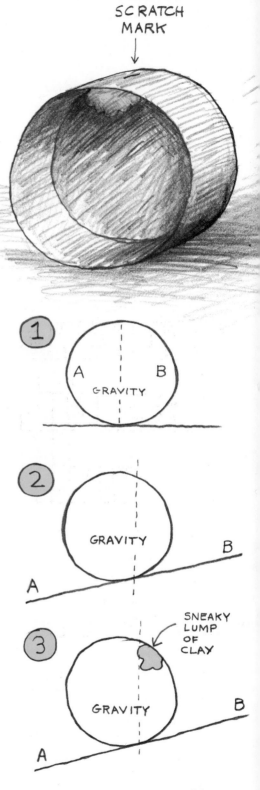

SCRATCH MARK

Downhill, of course. I'm going to cast a spell that will confuse this can so it will roll *uphill*. Now, watch what happens when I let this can go." You let the can go out of your hand and it indeed does what you say it will do—it rolls uphill!

How to Do It

Get a piece of board about three feet long and as wide as the can you are rolling is high. The can should have a tight-fitting lid. You'll also need a book about one-and-a-half-inches thick and a ball of modeling clay about the size of a Ping-Pong ball. Prepare the can in the following way before you show the trick to an audience: Stick the lump of clay inside the can—on the side, not the bottom—and put a scratch mark on the outside of the can where you've placed the clay. Put the lid on. You now know where the clay is; just find the scratch mark. Position the slat of wood so that one end rests on the book, forming a hill with a *slight* incline. (You may need to experiment in advance with the degree of incline.) Now, find the scratch mark, wave your hands mysteriously over the can, and say the magical words: Can Can Canada! Place the can on the board, about midway up. Before you let the can go, tilt the scratch mark slightly toward the top of the hill. The can will roll in that direction.

The Science Behind the Trick

Balance and gravity are at it again. Look at the diagram. When the can sits on a flat surface, it doesn't roll because gravity is pulling down on the A side and the B side evenly. The point where the can is touching the board is the balance point.

Now, look what happens when we make a slope. See how much of the can is being pulled down on the A side—more than half of the can. There's not

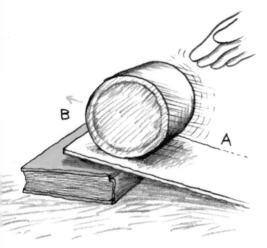

much of the can left on the B side to pull the other way. So, the can will naturally roll in the A direction—downhill.

That lump of clay stuck inside the can reverses the situation. Now, more of the weight is on the B side than the A side. Gravity pulls the clay down. That will make the can roll up the ramp a few inches—just far enough to fool your audience!

SLICING A PENCIL IN HALF

This is "magic" you can try on yourself right now. It will amaze you! You will hold an ordinary pencil between your hands and appear to slice it into two pieces, which are then moved apart. Of course, you don't really slice the pencil. There's a trick to this—and the trick is in your eyes! Once you catch on to how to do it correctly, you will be able to amaze your friends by showing them how they can do the magic, too. So get a pencil or a ballpoint pen and then do exactly what we tell you. . .

How to Do It

Put your palms together in front of you with your fingers straight up. Place a pencil between your fingers so that it pokes out on either side of your hands (see illustration).

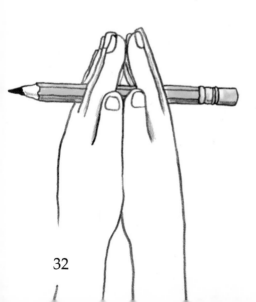

Now, stare at some object in the distance, like a picture hanging on a wall. Keep focusing on the object. Without changing your focus, move your hands up so they are between your eyes and the distant object. You will see your hands and the pencil, but they will look blurry because your eyes are not focused on them. Slide one hand downward about an inch. The pencil will appear to be sliced in half, with one end lower than the other. If this doesn't happen, it is because you have changed your focus. Do *not* focus on your hands; focus on the distant object.

When you've mastered the trick, slide your hand up and down and you'll find you can make the pencil appear to be either in one piece or broken.

The Science Behind the Trick

This is the type of trick called an *optical illusion*; it tricks your brain. Each of your eyes is like a tiny camera. It sees a separate picture, and because each eye is in a different place in your head, the picture each sees is slightly different. Your eyes send these different messages to your brain, telling it what they see. Your brain takes the two pictures and blends them together to make one picture. When you focus on a distant object and then hold the pencil close, both eyes see the distant object, but one eye sees one end of the pencil and the other eye sees the other end. When you slide one hand up or down, your brain is so busy making a single picture out of the *distant* object, it misses doing this with the close object, the pencil. One eye sees the pencil end go up, the other eye sees the other end go down. Your brain, busy with the distant object, doesn't put the pencil pictures together, so it is tricked into thinking that the pencil is broken.

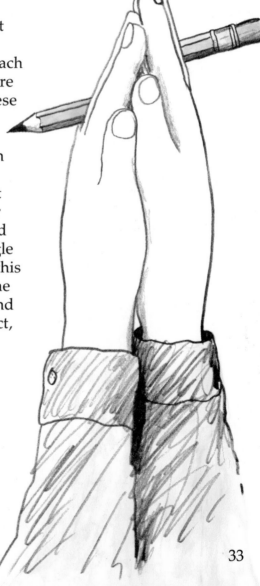

33

A nickel is placed on the table. A half-dozen pennies are placed on top of the nickel, forming a stack of coins. You are setting your audience up for a wonderful puzzle that you will solve with a bit of science magic.

As you stack the coins you tell this story: "I was in a grocery store last week and a customer stopped me, thinking I was a clerk. She brought me over to a stack of canned tomatoes. There was one big can on the very bottom of the stack of smaller cans. She told me that she wanted that big can, but she didn't dare to take it because she would topple over the entire stack. She wanted to know if I could help her get it."

Now, ask your audience to imagine that the pennies are the small cans of tomatoes and the nickel is the large can. Invite people to try to "help the lady" by getting the big can of tomatoes (the nickel) without unstacking the smaller cans (the pennies). And, to make everyone even more frustrated, say, "Well, naturally I helped the lady and she went home with the big can of tomatoes. I did it with a bit of science magic, and I didn't even touch any of the small cans." And then, before their very eyes, you show everyone how it's done!

How to Do It

Before you read about how this trick works, think for a moment. How would *you* get the nickel without touching or upsetting the pennies? The answer is simple, but maybe not obvious: you will use a bigger coin and will flick it, hard, against the nickel. Believe it or not, the nickel will scoot out from under the pennies and the pennies will stay stacked!

You'll need to get a quarter, in addition to your nickel and pennies. Call the quarter a "big canned ham" in your story. Set the quarter on the table about five inches away from the stack. Use your fingertip to flick the quarter, hard and fast, across the table so it hits the nickel. It will take a bit of practice, as in any magic trick, to learn to flick the quarter fast enough to hit the nickel. But when you do it right, the quarter will stop when it hits the nickel, and the nickel will be knocked out from under the stack. The stack will drop straight down onto the table without a penny being spilled. Just keep trying this trick until you are able to knock the nickel out every time. Then go and show off your "nickel knack" to everybody!

The Science Behind the Trick

When any object is sitting still, you know it won't start moving all by itself. The science term for an object's resistance to being moved is *inertia* (in-ER-sha). When a force is used against the object and is great enough to make that object move, we say that the force overcame the inertia. In this trick, the force of the quarter hitting the nickel is certainly great enough to overcome the inertia of the nickel. But, since the quarter does not even touch the pennies, there is no force great enough to overcome the inertia of the pennies.

35

PAPER CLIP FISHING

"Do you like to go fishing? Usually, all I catch is an old tire or a log, but one time I did catch a cold. And once, I had a fish catch *me*. I was playing cards at the time, and the fish was a card shark. But seriously, let's do a little fishing trick right now."

You bring out a paper cup that is half-filled with water and say, "This will be our ocean." Then show the audience four paper clips. "And these will be our fish." The paper clips are dropped into the cup.

"Now," you say, "your job is to fish out the paper clips, but you must do it without spilling the water or using anything to hook them. After all, this is a magic trick." When the people in your audience decide they can't accomplish this, you agree to do it instead. "But I will do it behind my back," you explain. You hold the cup behind your back and say, "How many fish would you like me to catch?"

The audience gives you a number—say, two. Almost immediately, you bring your hands forward. You are holding two paper clips! The other two clips are still submerged in the cup, and—most amazing—your hands are dry! You drop the two clips back into the water and hand the bottle to a spectator, saying, "That's how it's done. Now, let's see you take out just *one* fish!"

How to Do It

Fill a small paper cup about three-quarters full of water. You'll also need four paper clips and a strong magnet. Buy the magnet at a hardware store, hobby shop, or craft store. A small but strong magnet should cost less than a dollar; some will cost under fifty cents.

Drop the magnet into the back pocket of your pants, and you're all set. Hold the cup behind your back and take the magnet out of your pocket with the free hand. Place the magnet against the side of the cup, near the bottom, and tip the cup slightly toward the magnet, so that the clips are attracted to the magnet. Then, slide the magnet upward, keeping it pressed against the side of the cup. When the magnet reaches the edge of the cup, the clips will come out and cling to the magnet. All four clips will probably come out. By feel, you can count them. Just hold onto the number the audience asked for and drop any extras back into the cup.

Because you hide the magnet in your pocket again, you are ready to do the trick once more. But as with any good trick, don't do it so many times that people get bored with it.

The Science Behind the Trick

You already know that *magnetism* is the secret. A magnet has a north pole and a south pole. It can attract most metals. When it approaches another magnet, the north ends avoid each other, and the south ends avoid each other, but north and south are attracted to each other.

Particles in magnets are the shape of little tiny magnets themselves. The north ends of all these particles are pointing toward the north pole of the magnet while the south ends of the particles are pointing toward the magnet's south pole.

Why are some metals attracted to magnets? It's in their particles. As a magnet comes close, the metal's particles change shape, becoming little magnets, each with a north and a south pole. Remember that north and south attract each other. So, when you touch the north pole of your magnet to a piece of metal, the metal's particles point their south poles toward the magnet, and the two objects are pulled together.

PAPER CUP

MAGNET

37

WHERE'S THE GREEN?

IMADODO!

"I went to a magic show last week and the magician did a wonderful trick with a big glass of water and three small, empty glasses." You point to the four glasses on your table, one large and three small ones. The large one is full of clear water.

"The magician explained that he knew some secret words that would change the water to any color," you say as you pick up the large glass of water. "He asked the audience what color they would like, and they said, 'green.' The magician said that the magic word for green was 'Imadodo,' and when he poured the water into the empty glass, it would turn green." You pour water into one of the empty glasses. The water turns *red*!

"Red! Oh my, that is exactly what happened to that magician last week. Let me try again. Imadodo." You pour some water into the second small glass. It turns *blue*!

"Blue! Oh yes, that happened to the magician last week, too. But I'm a better magician than he was, and the third time never fails. Imadodo!" You pour water into the last glass; that water turns *yellow*!

"Yellow! My goodness, that didn't happen to the magician last week. Now I'm really confused! I guess I just don't know enough magic to turn the water green." You pour all three glasses back into the tall one. When you do, the water in the big glass turns green.

"Green! Oh no! Will somebody please explain this trick to me?"

How to Do It

This is a simple trick using special chemicals that are easy to obtain. In fact, you may have some in your kitchen right now. If not, you can buy them inexpensively at any grocery store. You will need three small bottles of food coloring—one red, one blue, and one yellow. These are liquids which can be added to certain foods, like cake frostings, to dye them pretty colors. You will also need a tall, clear glass and three small, clear glasses. The four glasses are set up this way:

The large glass is three-quarters full of plain water. In the first small glass, put one drop of red food coloring. In the second one, put one drop of blue food coloring. In the third one, put two drops of yellow food coloring. Set the small glasses in a row, next to the big glass. When you pick up each small glass, wrap your fingers around the bottom of the glass so the audience can't see the food coloring. To perform the trick, simply pour an equal amount of water into each of the small glasses. Then pour all of the water from the small glasses back into the large glass.

The Science Behind the Trick

How can one little drop of food coloring make a glass of water change its appearance? A drop of food coloring actually contains thousands of particles that can dissolve in the clear water. These colored particles are attracted to the water particles and therefore mingle throughout the water. The fact that there are so many particles in the food coloring also explains why you only need a few drops to color a whole batch of cake frosting.

This is a "'kitchen trick" because that's the best place to perform it. But you can do it elsewhere, too. Get one of the small plastic baskets that come from food stores and are filled with strawberries or other small fruits. (You might want to keep a basket on hand for whenever you want to pull this trick on a friend.)

You fill a big, clear bowl, or the sink, with water and hand the basket to the person you want to trick. "This basket," you tell your victim, "is made of a special plastic that will only float if you are a magician and have a very steady hand." Taking the basket from your victim, you demonstrate what you have just said. You place the basket very gently on the surface of the water, pretending to find it very hard to do, and finally let go of it. The basket, despite the fact that it is full of holes, floats on the water's surface. "If I did not have a steady, magical hand," you say, "and I jiggled the basket at all when I was setting it down . . ." you take hold of the top of the floating basket and wiggle it back and forth, ". . . it would have sunk immediately." As you let go, water pours through the holes in the basket, and it sinks to the bottom of the bowl or sink.

Now, you are set for some fun. Your friend has been tricked already, but he or she doesn't even suspect anything. "Do you know what?" you say. "I believe I am the only person I know who has a hand steady enough to do this." This, naturally, will make your friend anxious to prove you wrong.

Invite the friend to remove the basket and try. He or she might decide the basket has to be dry before starting. Give the friend a towel to dry it—the basket will still sink. It's fun to watch your friend try. Sometimes he or she will succeed in floating the basket for a few seconds. But, when the friend steps back—the basket will sink!

How to Do It

First, be sure you have the right kind of basket. It should have big, open squares. To test it, fill a bowl with fresh water and gently set the basket on top of the water. Without your really having to be extra careful, the basket will float. If you slosh it back and forth a bit so the water washes through the holes in the bottom, the basket will sink and stay submerged on the bottom of the bowl. Now, to make it impossible for your friend to perform the magic, you need an invisible element—dishwashing soap! Just put a tiny bit—a drop—of liquid soap on your fingertip and rub it around the very *top* edge of the basket. Be careful not to get any soap on the lower half or bottom of the basket or *you* won't be able to float the basket, either. Also, rinse your hands very well when you are done so no soap is left on you.

You are ready to present the trick, even hours after you rub soap on the basket. Your victim will never suspect what you've done.

The Science Behind the Trick

Water particles, like magnets, have north and south poles. The particles on the surface of water arrange themselves into a formation because of their attractions. Once these particles find their formation, they will not break apart easily. This formation is called *surface tension*. Because of surface tension, you can set the basket onto the water and it will float. If you break up the formation of particles, you lose the surface tension. Splashing the water does this. But that's too obvious for a magic trick. Soap is sneakier. It breaks up the special formation of water particles just by being put into the water. No special formation, no surface tension. The basket sinks. And, once the soap is in the water, the basket can't float again.

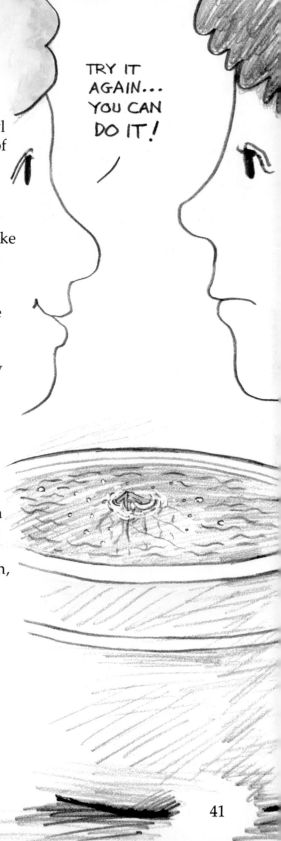

TRY IT AGAIN... YOU CAN DO IT!

HOW TO HYPNOTIZE A POTATO

On the table is a tall glass of water, a pencil, and a small potato. You say, "Ladies and gentlemen, I am an expert hypnotist. But I will not stand here and insult your intelligence by telling you I can hypnotize you. Instead, I am going to stand here and insult your intelligence by telling you I am going to hypnotize this potato!"

You pick up the potato and show it to the audience. "Don't laugh. All I have to do is stare the potato in its eyes!" You stare hard at the potato as though trying to hypnotize it and say, "You are under my spell and in my power . . . you will do exactly as I command you."

Turning to your audience, you gesture toward the glass of water. "Now, to demonstrate that the potato is hypnotized and will obey my every command, I will drop it in this glass of water. As you know, potatoes float in water." You stare at the potato. "But, *you*, my potato, will sink until I command you."

You put the potato carefully and slowly into the glass and, sure enough, it begins to sink. When it reaches the middle of the glass, you say, "Stop! I command you!" The potato stops, suspended halfway down the glass. Now, you poke the pencil into the glass and give the potato a little twirl as you say, "That's enough—the spell is now broken and you may float as you're supposed to." Slowly and magically, the potato rises upward and floats on the surface of the water.

YES MASTE I OBEY

42

How to Do It

This trick requires some special and careful preparation, but it's worth the time. People are very puzzled by it. To prepare your trick, start the night before your performance. First, fill a glass half-full of very hot water. Stir about half a cup of salt into the water. Place a small potato (or a piece of a potato) into the glass. If it floats, you have used enough salt. If it sinks, keep adding salt until the potato floats.

Once the potato floats, remove it and let the glass of salt water cool. The water will probably be cloudy because all of the salt is not dissolved. Let it sit overnight and the water will be clear. If some salt remains undissolved on the bottom, carefully pour the water into another glass, leaving the cloudy part behind.

The next step is a bit tricky. You must pour some fresh water into the glass until it is three-quarters full. Pour this water very, very slowly down the side of the glass, and the fresh water will float on top of the salt water without mixing with it. When you are done, you will not be able to see the difference between the salt water on the bottom and the fresh water above. You'll have what looks like a glass of ordinary water.

When you perform the trick, you first tell a little fib. You say, "As you know, potatoes float in water." People don't "know." If they did, they would know that potatoes *sink* in fresh water. But, they do float in salt water, and that is the trick's secret. Fresh water also floats on top of salt water, and that is part of the secret, too.

AS YOU KNOW, POTATOES FLOAT IN WATER

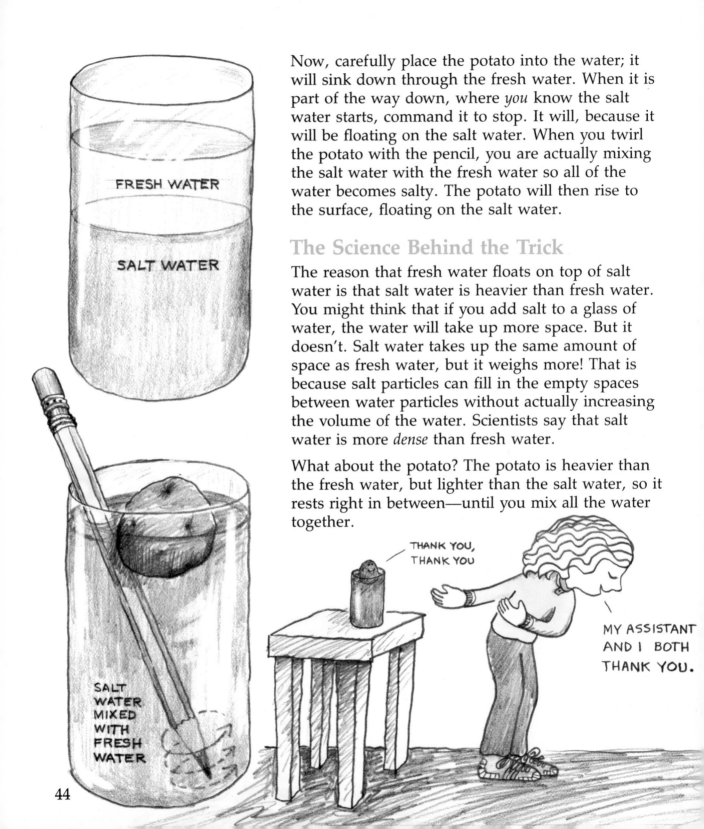

Now, carefully place the potato into the water; it will sink down through the fresh water. When it is part of the way down, where *you* know the salt water starts, command it to stop. It will, because it will be floating on the salt water. When you twirl the potato with the pencil, you are actually mixing the salt water with the fresh water so all of the water becomes salty. The potato will then rise to the surface, floating on the salt water.

The Science Behind the Trick

The reason that fresh water floats on top of salt water is that salt water is heavier than fresh water. You might think that if you add salt to a glass of water, the water will take up more space. But it doesn't. Salt water takes up the same amount of space as fresh water, but it weighs more! That is because salt particles can fill in the empty spaces between water particles without actually increasing the volume of the water. Scientists say that salt water is more *dense* than fresh water.

What about the potato? The potato is heavier than the fresh water, but lighter than the salt water, so it rests right in between—until you mix all the water together.

FRESH WATER

SALT WATER

SALT WATER MIXED WITH FRESH WATER

THANK YOU, THANK YOU

MY ASSISTANT AND I BOTH THANK YOU.

44

The science magician—that's you, now that you have read this book—is holding a large piece of cardboard and a marking pen. "Ladies and gentlemen, it has been my great pleasure to perform tricks for you. I hope I can do a show again real soon. Now my show is over, and I will write 'The End' on this piece of cardboard. Just so you won't forget who I am, I'll write my name, too, Oh, and to make sure you'll never forget how amazing I am, I will write both of these things *backwards* . . . and without looking!"

You hold the cardboard up in front of you, away from your body so only you can see the backside. Then, with the marking pen, you write on the *front* of the board:

THE END
YOUR NAME

What a neat way to end a science magic show!

How to Do It

This trick is ultra simple, but it takes a little practice. Once you've practiced, you can write anything you want backwards, without looking.

That's not really true; you *do* look. You look at the back of the cardboard! On the back, print in pencil (very lightly, in case your audience "accidentally" peeks) the words "THE END." Under it, write your name. Make all of the letters big so the audience will be able to see them when you write them on the other side.

Here's how you do that. Hold the cardboard with the pencil writing toward you, and look at the back. Hold the marker around the front of the card. Now simply pretend the cardboard is perfectly clear and you are looking right through it. Move the marker to the start and "trace" the letters on the other side of the cardboard! The audience sees you writing

THE END, BACKWARDS

45

backwards, but because *you* see the letters the right way around, you will find it simple to draw them on the other side of the card.

The Science Behind the Trick

We have saved the trick with the most amazing science "gimmick" for last. The gimmick is your *brain*. Think about it: without brains, there would be no science, none of these tricks would have been invented, and you would not be reading this book. Brains, we think, are the most magical things of all!

Your brain is able to control a hand in order to write marks called letters that other people can look at and understand with *their* brains. So, writing itself is pretty magical, but you make it look even more magical by writing your message backwards. With a little practice you will be able to do this trick without having anything already written on the cardboard. Just picture the words you want to write on the card, and "trace" your imaginary words onto the card's front side.

Your wonderful brain is capable of many things. We hope you have enjoyed using it in doing all of the tricks in this book.

ABOUT THE AUTHORS

Between the two of them, Larry White and Ray Broekel have about 60 years of science teaching. They've written around 300 books and have been doing tricks for around 110 years.

They've performed before many audiences, both young and old. In fact, many years ago, the authors did a magic show for the King of Siam. At least he told them he was. After the show was over he said, "Boy, if you guys are magicians, then I am the King of Siam."

Dr. Ray Broekel lives in Ipswich, Massachusetts. Among other things he was the Science Supervisor for *My Weekly Reader* for about ten years. Larry White lives in Stoughton, Massachusetts. He's the Director of the Science Center, Needham Public Schools, Needham, Massachusetts.

Meyer Seltzer has illustrated two other magic books for Larry White and Ray Broekel. He is the author and illustrator of two books, and illustrator of six other books for young readers. Mr. Seltzer was a good choice to illustrate this book because he believes that science *is* magic.

Mr. Seltzer is a graduate of the School of the Art Institute of Chicago, where his most amazing trick was disappearing from class.

DEMCO